Riyadh

A concise and Detailed Itinerary Handbook to a Memorable Adventure, Discovery and Insider's Experiences

BONUS:
- Itinerary
- Useful Phrases
- Family Vacation
- Solo Traveler
- Romantic Adventures
- Delectable Images

RIYADH
Travel Guide
2023

Elis Tello Rios

A concise and Detailed Itinerary handbook to a Memorable Adventure, Discovery and Insider's Experiences

Elis Tello Rios

Copyright 2023, Elis Tello Rios.

All Rights Reserved!

No part of this book may be reproduced, stored in a retrieval system, or transmitted in any form or by any means, electronic, mechanical, photocopying, recording, or otherwise, without the prior written permission of the copyright owner.

Table of Contents

INTRODUCTION..7

1.2 Purpose of this Guide............................. 10

Chapter 2: Essential Travel Information....... 12

2.1 Visiting Riyadh...12

2.2 Visa Requirements.................................. 13

2.3 Currency and Money Matters................. 14

2.4 Local Etiquettes and Customs.................15

2.5 Communication and Language..............16

Chapter 3: Getting to Riyadh........................18

Chapter 4: Accommodation Options............ 23

Chapter 5: Top Attractions in Riyadh..........28

Chapter 6: Cultural Experiences and Festivals... 34

Chapter 7: Outdoor Adventures and Nature......40

Chapter 8: Shopping and Entertainment..... 46

8.1 The Riyadh Shopping Malls....................46

8.2 Traditional Souvenirs and Crafts............47

8.3 Entertainment and Nightlife.................. 49

8.4 Activities for Families..............................51

8.5 Activities for Romantic Vacation............ 53

8.6 Guide for Solo Travelers........................... 54

Chapter 9: Insider's Tips &
Recommendations.. 57

9.1 Safety Measures... 57

9.2 The Ideal Season to Visit Riyadh............. 59

9.3 Local Tips and Hidden Gems.................. 60

9.4 Practical Arabic Phrases and
Pronunciations... 62

9.5 Helpful Contacts and Websites............... 65

9.6 Sustainable Tourism Practices................. 67

9.7 Suggested Itineraries................................. 69

Chapter 10: Conclusion............................... 75

10.1 Packing Checklist................................... 75

10.2 Recap of Riyadh Travel Guide.............. 77

10.3 Final Thoughts.. 78

5

INTRODUCTION

Welcome to Riyadh

Saudi Arabia's capital, Riyadh, is a compelling metropolis that skillfully combines heritage and innovation. This thriving city, located in the center of the Arabian Peninsula, is a center for trade, culture, and history. Riyadh embraces quick development and expansion while also showcasing a rich history with origins that go back many centuries.

As I landed in Riyadh, the energetic capital of Saudi Arabia, the sweltering desert wind blew over my hair. The city emanated an alluring mix of technology and a historical past, surrounded by imposing skyscrapers and classic architecture. I could feel the thrill and expectation for an incredible journey growing within me with each breath.

Walking through the busy streets, the enticing scent of freshly made coffee and Arabian spices filled the air. The streets were lined with vibrant kiosks that displayed a variety of traditional crafts and beautiful fabrics. Arabic music's rhythmic tunes flowed through the air, contributing to the sonic tapestry that portrayed the city's energetic mood.

I was in awe of the Al-Masmak Fortress, a glorious representation of the city's history, as I traveled to Riyadh's historical sites. Its deteriorated walls served as a reminder of the trials and victories of a bygone period. The vast National Museum, which was close by, drew attention with its promise of a fascinating tour through Saudi Arabia's rich history and culture.

However, Riyadh was a city that welcomed the future as well as the past. The Kingdom Centre Tower's contemporary design, which pierced the sky like a modern wonder, was evidence of the city's forward-thinking mentality. Riyadh provided a fascinating combination of old and new, appealing to every taste and inclination, from historic souks to modern retail complexes.

I realized that my voyage had only just started as the sun set and created a golden light over the city. With its outstanding attractions and gracious welcome, Riyadh offered me a multitude of discoveries and life-changing encounters. I excitedly anticipated the experiences that were ahead of me, anxious to experience the enchantment that lay inside this captivating Arabian city.

Riyadh is a metropolis that never sleeps, with tall buildings, vast shops, and first-rate services. A bustling mix of natives and foreigners populate its streets, fostering a global culture that is both exciting and friendly.

The striking architecture of the city—from the contemporary Kingdom Centre Tower to the historic Al-Masmak Fortress—serves as a physical reminder of its illustrious past and aspirational present.

1.2 Purpose of this Guide

This travel guide's objective is to provide visitors to Riyadh with a brief but comprehensive itinerary booklet. This book attempts to improve your experience whether you are a seasoned traveler or a first-time visitor by providing insightful observations, insider knowledge, and useful advice.

This travel guide is intended to be your traveling companion, helping you learn about the city's key sights and cultural events, as well as how to use public transit and find hidden treasures. To help you make the most of your time in Riyadh, it includes advice on places to stay, eat, buy, and be entertained.

Additionally, this guide explores the city's genuine experiences, regional festivals, and outdoor excursions to provide an unforgettable encounter. It strives to go beyond the typical tourist destinations, enabling you to experience Riyadh's genuine charm and authentic spirit.

This travel guide will act as your key to unlocking the finest of Riyadh, whether you're looking for ancient sites, bustling marketplaces, or exhilarating desert safaris. Get ready to go off on a voyage of exploration and make lifelong memories.

Chapter 2: Essential Travel Information

2.1 Visiting Riyadh

Through King Khalid International Airport (RUH), Riyadh has excellent connections to important cities all over the globe. International passengers may easily reach Riyadh because of the several airlines that run frequent flights there and back. Additionally, domestic aircraft link Riyadh with other Saudi Arabian cities.

If you want to travel by land, Riyadh has an efficient road system that makes it possible to get about by vehicle or bus. The city also boasts a rail system, with the Riyadh Metro linking different areas and offering effective citywide transit.

2.2 Visa Requirements

It's crucial to acquaint oneself with the visa procedures before departing for Riyadh. The majority of travelers to Saudi Arabia need a visa to enter the nation. Depending on your country of citizenship and reason for travel, the visa application procedure differs. For detailed visa criteria and procedures, it is advised to contact the Saudi Arabian embassy or consulate that is closest to you.

For qualified tourists, Saudi Arabia has introduced an electronic visa program known as the "eVisa". The visa enables a quicker and simplified application procedure for visas, making it more practical for travelers. It is advised to submit your eVisa application well in advance of the dates you want to visit.

2.3 Currency and Money Matters

The Saudi Riyal (SAR) is the country of Saudi Arabia's official currency. For daily spending, it is a good idea to have some local cash on hand, particularly when visiting markets or other smaller businesses that may not take foreign credit cards. Banks, exchange offices, and the airport all have currency exchange services accessible.

In Riyadh, there are several ATMs where you may use your foreign debit or credit card to withdraw money. Hotels, restaurants, and bigger retail outlets often take major credit cards like Visa and Mastercard. However, it's wise to always have some cash on hand in case a circumstance arises when cards aren't accepted.

2.4 Local Etiquettes and Customs

When visiting Riyadh, it's crucial to observe Saudi Arabian etiquette and respect local traditions. To remember, have the following in mind:

a) Be modest in your attire; Saudi Arabia has a strict dress code, especially for women. Dress modestly by covering your shoulders, and knees, and avoiding outfits that are too exposing.

b) Follow Local Religious Customs: Riyadh is an Islamic city, thus it's crucial to follow local cultural traditions. During the holy month of Ramadan, refrain from eating, drinking, or smoking in public and pay attention to prayer timings.

c) Gender segregation: There may be distinct zones for men and women in public places, including various modes of transportation. It's important to be informed about and respectful of these gender-specific traditions.

d) Public displays of affection: These kinds of demonstrations are impolite and need to be avoided.

2.5 Communication and Language

Arabic is the official language of Saudi Arabia. English is frequently employed in the commercial and tourist sectors, even though Arabic is widely spoken. Many employees who work in restaurants, hotels, and tourist locations are fluent in English.

It might be beneficial to learn a few fundamental Arabic words so that you can interact with the community and respect their culture. However, in tourist sites, both Arabic and English are accessible for the majority of signs and information.

In Riyadh, there is widespread mobile phone coverage, and several network providers provide international roaming services. In most hotels, eateries, cafés, and shopping centers, Wi-Fi is offered. To get inexpensive internet and voice services while visiting, think about buying a local SIM card for your smartphone.

By being acquainted with this crucial travel information, you'll be well-equipped to start your trip to Riyadh and move about the city with ease.

Chapter 3: Getting to Riyadh

3.1 Transportation Alternatives

You may choose from a variety of transportation choices to move to Riyadh depending on your interests and requirements. These include walking about the city, using public transit, taxis, ridesharing services, renting a vehicle, and driving yourself.

3.2 Public Transit

Buses and the subway make up the majority of Riyadh's effective and growing public transit system. With six lines that span different areas of the city, the Riyadh Metro offers a practical means to go from one neighborhood to the city's top sights. The metro is spotless, secure, and furnished with contemporary conveniences.

In Riyadh, there are also public buses that link the various parts of the city. Buses are an inexpensive alternative, however, they may not be as regular or as suitable for visitors as the metro system. It is a good idea to research bus routes and timetables beforehand.

3.3 Ridesharing and Taxi Services

In Riyadh, taxis are a widely used form of transportation. They are available at authorized taxi stands or may be flagged down on the street. Before beginning the trip, make careful to haggle over the fee or request that the driver utilize the meter. Taxis are easily accessible and provide a practical means of getting to certain locations.

In Riyadh, ride-hailing services like Uber and Careem are also commonly accessible. These transportation alternatives are practical and dependable, often with upfront pricing and the opportunity to monitor your route through a smartphone app.

3.4 Car Rental

If you want flexibility and freedom in your travels, renting a vehicle in Riyadh might be a practical choice. The city is home to several national and local automobile rental agencies. However, it's crucial to have a current driver's license and be knowledgeable about local traffic laws.

Since Riyadh has a well-established road system, driving around the city is not too difficult. To assist you navigate the streets, it is advised to utilize a GPS navigation system or a dependable map software on your smartphone.

3.5 Navigating the City

Since Riyadh is a large city, it might be difficult for first-time visitors to find their way around the many districts and attractions. Here are some pointers to get about the city:

a) Utilize maps and navigation tools on your smartphone to obtain instructions and map out your journey. Accurate instructions and up-to-date traffic information are offered through apps like Google Maps and Apple Maps.

b) Learn the location of important landmarks and significant thoroughfares in Riyadh. These may be used as landmarks to help you navigate the city.

c) Ask for instructions: Don't be shy about seeking advice or directions from locals, hotel personnel, or visitor information centers. The people of Saudi Arabia are renowned for their friendliness and willingness to assist.

You can travel about Riyadh comfortably and easily experience its numerous attractions and areas by being acquainted with the available transit choices and learning how to navigate the city.

Chapter 4: Accommodation Options

4.1 Hotels and Resorts

A variety of hotels and resorts are available in Riyadh to suit various needs and interests. Here are a few standout choices:

a) In the center of Riyadh, on King Fahd Road in the Olaya District, stands the opulent 5-star Burj Rafal Hotel. It provides classy accommodations, top-notch dining choices, a spa, and a rooftop pool with expansive city views.

b) Address: Al Hada Area, Makkah Road. The Ritz-Carlton, Riyadh is a well-known 5-star hotel recognized for its lavish lodgings, top-notch services, and gorgeous architecture. It has several dining options, a luxurious spa, and a lovely outdoor pool.

c) The five-star Four Seasons Hotel Riyadh is located in the renowned Kingdom Center Tower and provides opulent accommodations, superb cuisine, a rooftop pool, and a fitness center. Its address is Kingdom Center, King Fahd Road. It offers stunning views of the metropolitan skyline.

4.2 Guesthouses and Homestays

Guesthouses and homestays are great options for a more private and customized experience. While these lodging options may not be as prevalent in Riyadh as hotels, they do provide the opportunity to stay in a local home and enjoy Saudi hospitality. You may locate appropriate guesthouses and homestays in Riyadh through websites and platforms like Airbnb.

4.3 Budget-friendly Accommodations

Riyadh also offers a selection of comfortable, reasonably priced lodging options. These choices are appropriate for tourists on a limited budget. Here are a few illustrations:

a) Budget Hotel Al Yamama Palace - Al Nuzha (address: Al Nuzha, Riyadh) has tidy and welcoming rooms, a round-the-clock front desk, and free WiFi. It is conveniently situated close to major malls and tourist attractions.

b) The Orchid Hotel Riyadh is a cost-effective lodging option with standard features including cozy rooms, a restaurant, and free parking (address: Al Ghadir, Exit 8, Eastern Ring Road). It is conveniently located close to main highways for those who possess their vehicles.

c) Located in Al Falah, Riyadh, the Rest Night Hotel apartments - Al Falah offers roomy apartments with separate living rooms and kitchenettes. It is reasonably priced and situated in a neighborhood with convenient access to stores and eateries.

4.4 Choosing the Right Neighborhood

When choosing a place to stay in Riyadh, take your requirements into account when choosing a neighborhood. Here are a few well-liked areas:

a) Olaya: A thriving commercial area featuring a variety of five-star hotels, shops, and eateries. It is well-situated and provides quick access to a variety of attractions.

b) Al-Malaz: Popular for its parks and recreational facilities, Al-Malaz is a welcoming neighborhood for families with reasonably priced lodging and a laid-back vibe.

c) The Diplomatic Quarter is a posh district where many embassies, international organizations, and opulent hotels are located. It provides a tranquil setting with well-kept surroundings.

d) Al Hamra: This neighborhood in Riyadh's old district is home to classic architecture, hopping marketplaces, and cultural attractions. It offers an insight into the extensive history of the city.

e) When selecting an area, take into account elements like accessibility to attractions, available transit, and the community's vibe.

To get the greatest deals and availability, remember to plan and reserve lodging, particularly during busy travel times.

Chapter 5: Top Attractions in Riyadh

5.1 The Kingdom Center Tower

The Kingdom Centre Tower is one of Riyadh's most recognizable structures. This skyscraper, which has a height of 302 meters, has an observation deck on the 99th level that provides breathtaking views of the city. The skyscraper also features a posh retail center with companies from across the world, dining choices, and entertainment venues.

Address: Riyadh's Olaya Street

5.2 Al-Masmak Fortress

The historical fortification known as Al-Masmak was crucial in the formation of the Kingdom of Saudi Arabia. It offers a look into conventional Arabian architecture and sheds light on the lengthy history of the nation.

You may go around the museum inside, which has items and exhibitions relating to local history.

Address: Ad Dirah, Riyadh, Al-Imam Turki Ibn Abdullah Ibn Muhammad

5.3 National Museum

For fans of history and culture, the National Museum should not be missed. It provides a thorough voyage through Saudi Arabia's history, from the Paleolithic to the Modern Era. The museum's collections include relics from archaeology, manuscripts from antiquity, Islamic art, and interactive exhibitions that provide light on local traditions and customs.

King Faisal Road, Al Murabba, Saudi Arabia

5.4 Riyadh Zoo

Families and environment enthusiasts like visiting the Riyadh Zoo. The zoo, which covers more than 55 acres, is home to a wide variety of animals, including lions, giraffes, elephants, and birds.

Picnic places, strolls in the park, and educational activities focused on promoting animal conservation are available to visitors.

Address: Al Mathar Ash Shamali, Riyadh, Eastern Ring Road

5.5 Al-Bujairi Historical Village

A wonderful location that displays traditional Saudi Arabian architecture and cultural history is Al-Bujairi Historical Village. This rebuilt hamlet, which is situated along the banks of Wadi Hanifa, provides a look into the way of living in the past. Learn about the history and traditions of the area as you stroll through the modest museum, view the mud-brick structures, and explore the winding passageways. Visitors may immerse themselves in local culture by attending festivals and other cultural activities held in the town.

Address: Riyadh, Al-Dirah

5.6 Riyadh's Souks and Markets

For shoppers and visitors looking for a genuine cultural experience, Riyadh's souks and marketplaces are a gold mine. Here are some noteworthy marketplaces to check out:

a) Souk Al Zal: This vibrant market, which is well-known for its traditional textiles and crafts, sells a variety of goods, including carpets, ceramics, spices, and clothes.

b) Souk Al Zal Antique Market: This market has one-of-a-kind products including antique furniture, traditional jewelry, and historical antiques. It is a mecca for antique collectors and history aficionados.

c) The Souq Al Zal Carpet Market, which specializes in carpets and rugs, offers a huge variety of handmade carpets in both traditional and modern styles.

d) A haven for date lovers, the Souq Al Zal Dates Market provides a variety of fresh dates, date-related goods, and regional specialties created with dates.

Address: Several places around Riyadh

5.7 Diriyah Historical District

A must-visit location for history buffs is the UNESCO World Heritage Site known as the Diriyah Historical District. The first Saudi state was founded in this well-preserved neighborhood on the outskirts of Riyadh. Visit historical places, explore the mud-brick buildings, and discover more about the Al Saud dynasty. Additionally, Diriyah conducts festivals, exhibits, and cultural events that provide a window into Saudi Arabian traditions and customs.

Location: Riyadh, Diriyah
Al-Bujairi Historical Village, the bustling souks and marketplaces, and the old Diriyah quarter are just a few of the Riyadh attractions that provide a better knowledge of the history, culture, and customs of the area. Explore these alluring locations and immerse yourself in Saudi Arabia's rich history.

Chapter 6: Cultural Experiences and Festivals

6.1 Exploring Saudi Arabian Culture

Finding out about the traditions, customs, and values of the locals is made possible by exploring Saudi Arabian culture. Riyadh has several possibilities to explore the dynamic Saudi culture, including:

a) Visit the King Abdulaziz Historical Center, which houses the King Abdulaziz Historical Museum, King Abdulaziz Center for World Culture, and King Abdulaziz Library. These institutions provide information on the historical, artistic, literary, and scientific accomplishments of Saudi Arabia.

b) Discover the Heritage Village: The Heritage Village, which is a part of the King Abdulaziz Historical Center, has traditional architecture, handicrafts, and cultural exhibits. Craftspeople may be seen working on traditional crafts such as metals, weaving, and ceramics.

c) Attend cultural seminars: Keep an eye out for cultural events and workshops sponsored by community groups, museums, and art galleries. These classes provide participants the opportunity to practice Arabic language, calligraphy, traditional arts, and music.

6.2 Attending Cultural Events

A great approach to seeing local culture and seeing customs in action is to attend traditional events in Riyadh. Several things to think about are:

a) Camel Racing: This renowned Saudi Arabian classic sport is held on the outskirts of Riyadh. Watch how camels are led by their handlers over the tracks in the desert. It's an exhilarating and distinctive experience.

b) Falconry: The culture of Saudi Arabia has a strong foundation in falconry. To see trained falcons in action and learn about the art of falconry, you may go to falconry centers or events.

c) Watch out for cultural events that incorporate traditional music and dance performances, such as the Ardah dance, a classic Saudi Arabian sword dance. The intriguing rhythms and motions of the local culture may be enjoyed at these events.

6.3 Riyadh Season Festival

Annually, Riyadh hosts the Riyadh Season Festival, which features a wide variety of entertainment, cultural events, and activities. The festival features works by artists, musicians, and performers from throughout the world. You may take in live performances, art exhibits, gastronomic delights, and exhilarating amusement park rides. The event typically occurs in the colder months of the year and draws tourists from all around the globe.

6.4 Janadriyah Festival

On the outskirts of Riyadh, there is a significant cultural gathering called the Janadriyah Festival, also known as the Janadriyah National Heritage and Cultural Festival. It honors Saudi Arabia's cultural history and traditions. Folk dances, camel racing, horse displays, traditional crafts, and a variety of cultural events are all part of the festival. Visitors may learn about the rich history of Saudi Arabia via this comprehensive cultural experience.

6.5 Local Cuisine and Dining

Discovering the regional food is essential to understanding Riyadh's culture. The delicious fusion of tastes, spices, and distinctive dishes found in traditional Saudi Arabian cuisine is exquisite. Try some of these regional dishes:

a) Kabsa is an aromatic rice dish that is usually accompanied by soft meat, such as lamb or chicken and is topped with almonds and raisins.

b) Mandi: Another tasty rice dish, Mandi is often served with tender grilled chicken or beef and is prepared in a tandoor oven.

c) Mutabbaq: A tasty pastry stuffed with spicy meat or veggies, Mutabbaq is a well-liked street meal.

d) Arabian Coffee: Savor a cup of this rich, fragrant coffee, which is often served with dates, to experience Saudi Arabia's legendary hospitality.

e) Local Candies: Indulge in classic Saudi Arabian candies like Baklava, Luqaimat (sweet dumplings), and Basbousa (semolina cake drenched in syrup).

In Riyadh, you may discover regional eateries, cafés, and food markets to get a taste of the cuisine and hospitality of Saudi Arabia.

Chapter 7: Outdoor Adventures and Nature

7.1 The Edge of the World

Just outside of Riyadh lies the stunning natural wonder known as The Edge of the World. Stunning cliffs that loom over a broad desert plain are part of this geological formation. The magnificent vistas and unending horizon may be appreciated while standing at the edge, inspiring awe and amazement. It's the ideal location for taking pictures, going on a hike, or just admiring the beauty of the desert surroundings.

Location: Riyadh, Ushaiger - Al Hofuf Road

7.2 Wadi Hanifa

Northwest of Riyadh is where you'll find the gorgeous valley known as Wadi Hanifa. This desert paradise is renowned for its unspoiled beauty, luxuriant vegetation, and meandering waterways. Numerous leisure activities, including hiking, bicycling, and picnics, are available in the vicinity. Along the length of Wadi Hanifa, several parks provide peaceful places to unwind and take in beautiful surroundings.

Address: Riyadh, Wadi Hanifa

7.3 Parks and Gardens in Riyadh

Many parks and gardens can be found around Riyadh, giving locals and guests access to outdoor areas and recreational opportunities. Here are a few of Riyadh's well-liked parks:

a) King Fahd Park is one of Riyadh's biggest parks and is home to lovely gardens, strolling walkways, fountains, and play spaces. Additionally, it provides lake boat excursions in the park. (King Fahd Park: Riyadh's Al Malaz)

b) Salam Park is a large, kid-friendly park with playgrounds and picnic places that is situated right in the middle of Riyadh. Additionally, it holds several occasions and exhibits all year round. (Salam Park: Riyadh, as Salam)

c) Al-Malaz Park: With a zoo, amusement attractions, and recreational amenities, Al-Malaz Park is a well-liked vacation spot for families. It's a wonderful location for kids to engage in outdoor activities and interact with animals.

Address: Al-Malaz Park: Riyadh's Al-Malaz

7.4 Days Trips from Riyadh

The proximity of Riyadh to several fascinating day trip locations makes them accessible. From Riyadh, some well-liked choices for day excursions are as follows:

a) Explore the historical district of Diriyah, a UNESCO World Heritage site, and its historic buildings, museums, and other cultural attractions.

b) Al Ula: About 900 kilometers to the northwest of Riyadh, Al Ula is renowned for its outstanding ancient monuments, including

Madain Saleh (Al-Hijr), which is included on the UNESCO World Heritage List.

c) The Edge of the World is a breathtaking natural site that provides panoramic views of the desert environment, as was previously described.

d) Red Sands (Ad Diriyah Desert): Experience the exhilaration of desert activities like sandboarding, camel riding, and dune buggying at the Red Sands desert, which is close to Riyadh.

7.4 Desert Safaris and Camel Riding

In Riyadh, camel rides and desert safaris are well-liked outdoor pursuits that let guests feel the allure of the Arabian desert. Many tour companies provide an opportunity to explore the dunes, see captivating sunsets, and take part in traditional Bedouin hospitality via guided camel rides and desert safari excursions. These pursuits are a great opportunity to see the desert's culture firsthand and have unforgettable experiences.

Reputable tour companies that put animal welfare first and use ethical, sustainable techniques are advised to be used when booking outdoor activities and desert safaris.

Chapter 8: Shopping and Entertainment

8.1 The Riyadh Shopping Malls

Modern, large retail centers in Riyadh are renowned for their diverse selection of national and international brands, leisure activities, and eating establishments. Listed below are a few prominent malls in Riyadh:

a) Kingdom Centre Mall: This upmarket mall is housed within the well-known Kingdom Centre Tower and offers high-end shops, designer boutiques, and luxury brands. Additionally, it has upscale eating establishments and a Sky Bridge with a panoramic view of the city.

b) Al Nakheel Mall is a well-liked spot for shopping and leisure because of its distinctive style, which was inspired by palm trees. It has a wide range of retail establishments, a food court, a theater district, and a sizable indoor amusement park.

c) **Riyadh Gallery Mall:** This shopping center is renowned for its eclectic mix of national and international brands, as well as for offering a wide range of food establishments. A kids' play area and entertainment areas are also included.

d) **Panorama Mall:** This popular shopping destination is home to a variety of high-street fashion labels, electronics retailers, and gourmet cuisine establishments. Additionally, it sometimes hosts events and exhibits.

8.2 Traditional Souvenirs and Crafts

Visit traditional marketplaces and specialty shops in Riyadh for genuine Saudi Arabian mementos and handicrafts. Some things to watch out for are:

a) Saudi Arabia is well known for its delectable dates. Various dates, such as Ajwa, Sukkari, or Khalas, as well as packaged date items that make wonderful presents should be on your shopping list.

b) Oud and perfumes: In Arabian culture, the aromatic resin known as oud is highly prized. Investigate boutiques and perfumeries that sell a variety of incense, fragrances, and other fragrant items made with oud.

c) Take home an authentic Arabic coffee set, which usually consists of a dallah (coffee pot) and tiny cups. These sets often include lovely, complex decorations.

d) Consider buying some traditional Saudi Arabian attire, such as a thobe (robe) for men or an abaya (cloak) for women, to get a feel for the country's culture.

Look for handmade products including ceramics, carpets, rugs, woven baskets, and silver jewelry, which highlight Saudi Arabia's creative talent and cultural history.

8.3 Entertainment and Nightlife

Even though Riyadh is renowned for its strict social climate, tourists may still find entertainment and nightlife alternatives there. These consist of:

a) Riyadh has a wide variety of eateries, serving anything from local cuisine to delicacies from across the world. Additionally, several places provide cultural programs or live music in the evenings.

b) Keep up current on cultural activities that take place at locations like the King Fahd Cultural Center or the King Abdulaziz Center for World Culture (Ithra), such as musical performances, art exhibits, theatrical productions, and poetry recitals.

c) Theme Parks: Have fun with the family in amusement parks with rides, arcades, and other fun things to do like Al Hokair Land or Granada Center.

d) Sporting and Recreation: There are several sporting facilities and clubs in Riyadh where you may relax or indulge in physical activity, including golf courses, fitness centers, and bowling alleys.

e) Entertainment choices at hotels include live music, DJs, and themed evenings in the lounges and nightclubs of several opulent hotels in Riyadh.

It's crucial to remember that Riyadh's nightlife and entertainment alternatives follow regional laws and traditions.

Always examine the exact laws and regulations for such places' dress requirements, drink policies (alcohol is often not permitted in public settings), and gender segregation policies.

8.4 Activities for Families

Family-friendly activities for guests of all ages are available in Riyadh. Here are a few possibilities:

a) Riyadh Zoo: View a variety of creatures from across the globe at the Riyadh Zoo. The zoo offers a petting zoo, animal displays, and educational exhibits.

b) Al Hokair Land is a well-known amusement park featuring exciting rides, arcades, and family-friendly entertainment.

c) Explore the King Fahd Cultural Center, which presents exhibits, performances, and courses with an emphasis on the arts, sciences, and culture. It also features a sizable park with kid-friendly play areas.

d) King Abdullah Park is a sizable park with lovely landscaping, strolling trails, play spaces, and picnic places. It also conducts seasonal events and rents out boats on its lake.

e) Bowling and Laser Tag: Have family-friendly fun at places like Sparky's, which has bowling, laser tag, and arcade games.

8.5 Activities for Romantic Vacation

Riyadh offers possibilities for romantic getaways that may provide unforgettable experiences for couples. Here are some recommendations:

a) Al Malaz Horse Racing Track: Go horse racing for the evening at Al Malaz Horse Racing Track, where you may root for your favorite athletes and take in the exciting ambiance.

b) Take a romantic boat trip along the lovely Wadi Hanifa while taking in the serene surroundings and breathtaking vistas.

c) Sunset at the Edge of the World: Take in the spectacular sunset against the enchanting desert scenery at the Edge of the World.

d) Riyadh has a wide selection of fine dining establishments that include romantic surroundings and delectable food. For a memorable evening, look for restaurants with rooftop views or outdoor seats.

e) Couples Spa Experience: Treat your significant other to a relaxing couples spa treatment at one of the city's upscale facilities.

8.6 Guide for Solo Travelers

Here are some pointers and advice for lone visitors to Riyadh:

a) Take standard safety measures, such as maintaining vigilance in public locations, avoiding secluded regions at night, and securing your possessions.

b) Respect for local traditions and customs, modest attire, and adherence to Saudi Arabian cultural standards are all examples of cultural sensitivity. Learn the manners and traditions of the area to guarantee a courteous and easygoing visit.

c) Join Guided Tours: To learn more about the city, think about taking a guided tour or hiring a local guide. This may provide information on the culture, history, and way of life in the area.

d) Experience Saudi Arabian culture firsthand by visiting museums, cultural institutions, and historical places. They provide chances to discover the history, culture, and customs of the nation.

e) Join local interest organizations or attend social gatherings to interact with the community. You may also attend cultural seminars. You may learn more about the city and its residents as a result.

f) Enjoy Solo Activities: Riyadh provides a variety of solo traveler-friendly activities, such as strolling casually around the city or enjoying parks, marketplaces, and local food.
Traveling alone in Riyadh may be a great experience since it gives you the freedom to explore the city at your speed and take in all of its distinctive beauty.

Chapter 9: Insider's Tips & Recommendations

9.1 Safety Measures

Prioritizing safety is crucial while visiting Riyadh. Here are some things to remember about safety:

a) Respect Local Laws and traditions: Make sure you are following local laws and traditions by becoming familiar with them. Respect cultural sensibilities, dress modestly, and observe regional traditions.

b) Take steps to keep your possessions safe while touring the city and keep valuables locked up. In busy places, keep costly stuff hidden and watch out for pickpockets. Put your valuables in the hotel safes.

c) Keep Up with Travel Warnings: Before leaving for Riyadh, check to see whether your country's embassy or consulate has issued any travel warnings or advisories. Keep up with local circumstances, and abide by any safety advice or rules.

d) Use Reliable Transportation: When moving throughout the city, use trustworthy ride-hailing services or apps. Use well-known and reliable transportation choices, and be sure the car has the right license.

e) Be Aware of Your Environment: At all times, be vigilant and mindful of your surroundings. Avoid going for solitary strolls in remote regions, especially at night. When possible, stay in well-lit, crowded locations.

9.2 The Ideal Season to Visit Riyadh

The winter months of November through March are the ideal time to visit Riyadh since the weather is gentler and more conducive to outdoor activities. The winter months are comfortable, with daily highs of 20°C to 25°C (68°F to 77°F) and colder nighttime lows. Expect greater crowds and more expensive accommodation rates as this is also the busiest travel season.

Avoid traveling to Riyadh in the summer (June to September), when humidity levels are high and temperatures may reach over 40°C (104°F), making outdoor activities difficult. You may still travel during this period as long as you take appropriate heat-related measures if your plans include seeing indoor sights or taking advantage of cheaper accommodation prices.

9.3 Local Tips and Hidden Gems

Here are some insider tips and undiscovered treasures to discover in Riyadh to help you make the most of your trip there:

a) Al Zal Historical District: Visit the Al Zal neighborhood, which is in the center of Riyadh's old town, to see the traditional architecture, winding lanes, and historical structures. It offers an insight into the extensive history of the city.

b) Al-Masmak Street Market: Explore a classic open-air market by going to the Al-Masmak Street Market, which is close to the Al-Masmak Fortress. It provides a variety of products, including handicrafts, spices, textiles, and souvenirs.

c) Discover the Al Rawdah Local Market, which is renowned for its seasonal food, regional honey, and traditional Saudi Arabian goods. It offers a genuine and lively shopping experience.

d) Wadi Hanifa Walkway: Take a stroll along this picturesque promenade that follows the route of Wadi Hanifa. Enjoy the rich vegetation and tranquil ambiance as you stroll or ride a bike along the track.

e) Visit the famous Ad Diriyah Oasis, an ancient oasis that is situated in the Diriyah neighborhood. Discover the mud-brick architecture and palm groves while learning about the area's past.

f) Local Cuisine: Don't pass up the chance to sample real Saudi Arabian food in neighborhood eateries and food carts. Try some of the country's traditional cuisine, including Mandi, Kabsa, and sweets like Kunafa and Qatayef.

You may dig deeper into the real culture, history, and tastes of Riyadh by discovering these local secrets, making your trip more immersive and unforgettable.

9.4 Practical Arabic Phrases and Pronunciations

- ★ Hello - Marhaba (mar-ha-ba)
- ★ Good morning - Sabah al khair (sa-bah al-khair)
- ★ Good evening - Masaa al khair (ma-sa al-khair)
- ★ Thank you - Shukran (shook-ran)
- ★ Yes - Naam (na-am)
- ★ No - Laa (la)
- ★ Please - Min fadlak (min fad-lak) - when speaking to a male
- ★ Please - Min fadlik (min fad-lik) - when speaking to a female

★ Excuse me - Law samaht (law sa-maht)

★ I'm sorry - Ana asif (a-na a-sif)

★ Do you speak English? - Tatakallam al-Ingleeziya? (ta-ta-kal-lam al-in-glee-zee-ya)

★ Where is...? - Ayna...? (ay-na)

★ How much does it cost? - Kam thamanahu? (kam tha-ma-na-hu)

★ Can you help me? - Hal tasta'tee al-musa'adah? (hal tas-ta-tee al-mu-sa-a-da)

★ I don't understand - Ana laa afham (a-na la af-ham)

★ What is your name? - Ma ismuka? (ma is-moo-ka) - when speaking to a male

★ What is your name? - Ma ismuki? (ma is-moo-ki) - when speaking to a female

★ Where is the bathroom? - Ayna al-hammam? (ay-na al-ham-mam)

★ Can I have the check, please? - Mumkin al-hisab min fadlak/fadlik? (mum-kin al-he-sab min fad-lak/fad-lik)

★ Goodbye - Ma'a as-salamah (ma-a as-sa-la-mah)

Note: Dialect may affect how Arabic is spoken. The pronunciations provided serve as a general reference.

9.5 Helpful Contacts and Websites

Here are some useful phone numbers and URLs for your trip to Riyadh:

a) Dial 999 for police, 997 for an ambulance, and 998 for fire services in the event of an emergency.

b) Embassy/Consulate: For guidance and support during your visit, get in touch with the embassy or consulate of your nation in Riyadh.

c) General Authority for Tourism and National Heritage: The official Saudi Arabian tourism website offers information on destinations, activities, and travel advice. Visit the Saudi Tourism website.

d) Visit Riyadh: The city's official tourist website provides comprehensive information about its sights, lodging options, cuisine, and events. visitriyadh.com is the website.

d) Riyadh Metro: Information about routes, prices, and timetables may be found on Riyadh Metro's official website. theriyadhmetro.sa website

e) Saudi Arabian Airlines: Saudi Arabian Airlines (Saudia) is the country's flag airline and provides both local and international services. Web address: saudia.com

f) Uber and Careem are two well-known ride-hailing services that are accessible in Riyadh. Get the corresponding applications for easy transportation.

g) Before your journey, it's a good idea to check for the most recent updates and contact data since websites and phone numbers are subject to change.

9.6 Sustainable Tourism Practices

Using sustainable travel practices reduces your environmental effect and benefits the neighborhood when you visit Riyadh. Here are some suggestions for eco-friendly travel:

a) Respect the environment by using the appropriate paths, not leaving trash behind, and properly disposing of garbage. Respect wildlife by keeping a safe distance from it and its environment.

b) Use water and energy resources appropriately to conserve both. Reduce water use, switch off devices and lights when not in use, and save energy in lodgings.

c) Choose locally owned hotels, eateries, and retail establishments to support the neighborhood economy. Directly from local artists and craftsmen, you may purchase souvenirs and handmade items.

d) Participate in responsible tourism by learning about regional traditions and customs and observing cultural sensitivity. Dress modestly, get permission before snapping pictures of individuals, and behave respectfully while interacting with the neighborhood.

e) Reduce Plastic trash: Use reusable water bottles, and eco-friendly shopping bags, and steer clear of single-use plastics to reduce plastic trash.

f) Use Public Transportation or Shared Rides: To cut down on carbon emissions and traffic, consider using public transportation or ridesharing services. Use the Riyadh Metro for quick, sustainable transit across the city.

You may aid in the preservation of Riyadh's natural and cultural legacy and have a pleasant and responsible trip by implementing these sustainable travel habits.

9.7 Suggested Itineraries

Cultural Delights

Day 1:

- Start the day by exploring Saudi Arabia's rich history and cultural heritage at the National Museum.

- Discover the historical importance of the Al-Masmak Fortress, which is where the Kingdom of Saudi Arabia was founded.

- Wander around the bustling Al Zal Historical District's congested streets, taking in the local culture and architecture as you go.

- Take a walk in the evening along the Wadi Hanifa Walkway to take in the scenery and tranquility of the oasis.

Day 2:
- Explore the King Abdulaziz Library, the King Abdulaziz Center for World Culture (Ithra), and the King Abdulaziz Historical Museum at the King Abdulaziz Historical Center throughout the morning.

- Visit a nearby restaurant for a classic Saudi Arabian meal.

- Visit the Al-Bujairi Historical Village in the afternoon to take in the traditional Saudi Arabian architecture, handicrafts, and cultural exhibits.

- Attend a traditional music and dance performance or a cultural workshop to round off the day.

Modern Marvels:

Day 1:

- Go to the renowned Kingdom Centre Tower first thing in the morning. Explore the opulent mall while admiring the mesmerizing views of Riyadh from the observation deck.

- Visit the Riyadh Gallery Mall for some shopping therapy and a satisfying lunch at one of the numerous restaurants there.

- Visit the King Fahd Cultural Center in the afternoon for an immersive and instructive experience where you may immerse yourself in cultural, scientific, and artistic displays.

- Take a stroll around King Fahd Park to unwind at the end of the day while seeing the lovely flowers and park facilities.

Day 2:
- Explore the bustling Souq Al Zal and Souq Al Zal Antique Market first thing in the morning to discover local handicrafts, clothing, and interesting antiquities.

- Visit the Souk Al Zal Carpet Market and the Souk Al Zal Dates Market to take in the vibrant atmosphere while shopping for high-quality carpets and indulging in some of Saudi Arabia's world-famous dates.

- At a nearby restaurant, take advantage of a typical Saudi lunch and appreciate the cuisine.
- Spend the evening in Al-Malaz Park, where you can take strolls, explore the zoo, and make use of the park's recreational amenities.

Nature and Adventure:

Day 1

- Go on an amazing desert safari and take part in sandboarding, camel riding, and dunking in the Red Sands (Ad Diriyah Desert).

- Experience the friendliness of the Bedouin people while taking in a traditional Arabian meal beneath the stars in a desert tent.

Day 2:

- Discover the spectacular Edge of the World and be in awe of the majestic cliffs and expansive desert vistas.

- Visit Wadi Hanifa to enjoy outdoor pursuits like cycling or hiking along the lovely promenade.

- At a nearby spa, relax while taking advantage of wellness activities and rejuvenating therapies.

You may use these recommended itineraries as a jumping-off point for your tour of Riyadh and alter them to suit your tastes and interests. Don't forget to take into account the location's accessibility, the availability of transportation, and any upcoming events or festivals.

Chapter 10: Conclusion

10.1 Packing Checklist

Here is a packing list to make sure you have everything you need for your trip before I wrap up the Riyadh travel guide:

- aA current passport and other essential travel documentation
- Visa, if necessary
- Saudi Riyal, local currency, or credit or debit cards
- Comfortable attire that is in keeping with the season and regional traditions
- For trips to religious locations, dress modestly (in loose-fitting garments that cover the shoulders and knees).
- Footwear that is appropriate for walking and outdoor activities
- For sun protection, use a hat, sunscreen, and sunglasses.

- For chilly nights, a lightweight jacket or sweater
- Electrical travel adaptor (Type G plugs are used in Saudi Arabia)
- Medication and any prescriptions that may be required
- Medical kit
- Items for personal care and toiletry
- Face masks and hand sanitizer in portable sizes
- Books about travel or offline maps
- Using a camera or smartphone to record memories
- A power bank or portable charger for your electronic gadgets
- Information about travel insurance and emergency numbers
- Don't forget to pack for the season and the activities you have planned while there.

10.2 Recap of Riyadh Travel Guide

This Riyadh Travel Guide offered a thorough schedule for an unforgettable journey in Saudi Arabia's capital city. It includes crucial details including packing advice, visa needs, regional traditions, and fundamental language skills.

The guide discussed various modes of transportation, lodging alternatives, and prominent sights such as the Kingdom Centre Tower, Al-Masmak Fortress, and Riyadh Zoo. It also highlighted natural attractions like the Edge of the World and Wadi Hanifa as well as cultural events, festivals, shopping, and entertainment.

The guide provided advice on romantic getaways, family-friendly activities, and suggestions for lone travelers. It placed a focus on environmentally conscious transport methods that also benefit the neighborhood.

10.3 Final Thoughts

We hope that our travel guide has given you the knowledge and suggestions you need as your trip to Riyadh draws near so that it will be a memorable one. Riyadh has something for everyone, whether you want to see historical monuments, indulge in regional cuisine, or fully immerse yourself in cultural activities. Consider practicing sustainable travel wherever you can, paying attention to safety considerations, and respecting local traditions.

Printed in Great Britain
by Amazon